HOLIDAY JOKES & SWEET TREATS

APRIL FOOLS' DAY SNICKERS & SNACKS

Anna Anderhagen

Consulting Editor, Diane Craig, MA/Reading Specialist

Super Sandcastle

An Imprint of Abdo Publishing
abdobooks.com

abdobooks.com

Published by Abdo Publishing, a division of ABDO, PO Box 398166, Minneapolis, Minnesota 55439. Copyright © 2025 by Abdo Consulting Group, Inc. International copyrights reserved in all countries. No part of this book may be reproduced in any form without written permission from the publisher. Super Sandcastle™ is a trademark and logo of Abdo Publishing.

Printed in the United States of America, North Mankato, Minnesota
102024
012025

THIS BOOK CONTAINS RECYCLED MATERIALS

Design: Layne Halvorsen, Mighty Media, Inc.
Production: Mighty Media, Inc.
Editor: Liz Salzmann
Cover Photographs: Mighty Media, Inc. (recipe photos); Shutterstock Images
Interior Photographs: Adobe Stock, pp. 4–5 (children), 8 (dates), 9 (litter scoop, brownies, tray), 11 (chocolate chips), 12 (hands), 13 (containers, washing plate), 29 (litter scoop), 30 (joker); Mighty Media, Inc. (recipe photos), pp. 9, 10, 14, 15, 16, 17, 18, 19, 20, 21, 22, 23, 24, 25, 26, 27, 29; Shutterstock Images, pp. 1 (rolling pin), 6 (all), 7 (child), 8 (Oreos, food coloring), 8–9 (graham crackers, Nutella, sugar), 9 (Q-tips, parchment paper), 11 (almond bark, caramel), 14 (child), 16 (child), 20 (cat), 22 (cockroaches), 24 (rocks), 28–29 (child), 29 (plate, rolling pin), 30 (rabbit), 31 (children)
Design Elements: Shutterstock Images (abstract doodles, kitchen utensil doodles)

Library of Congress Control Number: 2024938351

Publisher's Cataloging-in-Publication Data
Names: Anderhagen, Anna, author.
Title: April Fools' Day snickers & snacks / by Anna Anderhagen
Description: Minneapolis, Minnesota : ABDO Publishing, 2025 | Series: Holiday jokes & sweet treats | Includes online resources and index.
Identifiers: ISBN 9781098295172 (lib. bdg.) | ISBN 9798384915225 (ebook)
Subjects: LCSH: Jokes--Juvenile literature. | April Fools' Day--Juvenile literature. | Pranks--Juvenile literature. | Holidays--Juvenile literature. | Snack foods--Juvenile literature. | Cooking--Juvenile literature.
Classification: DDC 398.7--dc23

TO ADULT HELPERS

The sweet treats in this series are fun and simple. There are just a few things to remember to keep kids safe. Creating some treats requires the use of hot objects. Also, kids may be using messy materials, such as food coloring. Make sure they protect their clothes and work surfaces. Review the projects before starting and be ready to assist when necessary.

Super Sandcastle™ books are created by a team of professional educators, reading specialists, and content developers around five essential components—phonemic awareness, phonics, vocabulary, text comprehension, and fluency—to assist young readers as they develop reading skills and strategies and increase their general knowledge. All books are written, reviewed, and leveled for guided reading and early reading intervention programs for use in shared, guided, and independent reading and writing activities to support a balanced approach to literacy instruction.

Contents

April Fools' Day............. 4

Holiday Hoots!.............. 6

Sweet Materials............. 8

Melting Tips & Tricks........ 10

Treats Prep................ 12

Dirty Earwax Cotton Swabs.. 14

Sweet Mini Burger Surprise.. 16

Cat Poop Cookies........... 20

Cockroach Crunchies........ 22

Cookies & Cream Rocks...... 24

Keep Creating!............. 28

Last Laughs................ 30

Glossary................... 32

APRIL FOOLS' DAY

Have you ever played an April Fools' Day **prank** on someone? Or have you had one played on you? If so, you aren't alone. People have **celebrated** April Fools' Day in different **cultures** for hundreds of years.

No one knows for sure how the holiday started. Some **historians** say it comes from the ancient Roman **festival** Hilaria. During Hilaria, people dressed up in costumes to fool one another. By the late 1500s, people in France had begun placing paper fish on other people's backs and calling them *Poisson d'avril*. This means "April fish."

April Fools' Day **traditions** today include playing **practical jokes** and then saying "April Fools!" On April Fools' Day, some companies and websites play tricks too. For example, Internet company Google introduced Google Nose on April Fools' Day. It claimed to let people search for smells online. But it was a prank!

Why do eggs like April Fool's Day?

They are full of practical yolks!

5

Holiday Hoots!

What did the tree say when April finally arrived?

What a re-leaf.

On April Fools' Day, how many tickles does it take to make an octopus laugh?

Ten-tickles!

What day of the year do monkeys go bananas?

The first of Ape-ril!

What did the hammer say to the wrench on April 1?

Happy April Tools' Day!

What did the bread do on spring break?

It loafed around.

On April Fools' Day, what's the best time to go to the dentist?

Tooth-hurty.

What do you call a bear caught in the rain on April 1?

A drizzly bear!

What is a gas pump's favorite holiday?

April Fuels' Day!

I am in the middle of both March and April, but not at the beginning or end. What am I?

The letter *r*.

Sweet Materials

Here are some of the ingredients and tools you will need to make the treats in this book.

Ingredients

- chocolate brownies
- chocolate frosting
- chocolate hazelnut spread
- cocoa powder
- food coloring
- graham crackers
- Haribo Sour Streamers (orange)
- Hot Tamale candies
- mini marshmallows
- Oreo cookies
- pitted dates
- powdered sugar
- pretzel sticks
- shredded coconut
- soft caramel squares
- strawberry Pocky sticks
- sweetened condensed milk
- vanilla almond bark
- vanilla wafers

What do you call a train full of caramel?

A chew-chew train.

Tools

- baking sheet
- cotton swabs
- knife & cutting board
- measuring cups
- microwave-safe bowl
- new, clean kitty litter scoop
- parchment paper
- rolling pin
- sealable plastic bags
- shallow foil pan
- tray

What is the smartest tool?
A thermometer because it has so many degrees.

Melting Tips & Tricks

Some of the recipes in this book require you to melt ingredients in the microwave. To melt means to heat something until it is soft or liquid. Here are some tips for melting success!

General Tips

- Put the ingredient in a microwave-safe bowl.
- Microwave for 20 seconds at a time.
- Stir after each time. If you don't, the ingredient could burn.
- Repeat until the ingredient becomes creamy and smooth.

Did you hear about the baker who accidentally backed into an open oven?
His buns were toasted!

Extra Tips for Caramel

* Use soft caramel squares, not hard caramel candies.
* Unwrap the caramels before microwaving them.

> How did the small oven greet the large oven?
>
> **It micro-waved.**

Extra Tip for Almond Bark

* Cut the almond bark into small **chunks**. Smaller chunks will melt more quickly.

Extra Tips for Chocolate Chips

* Make sure the microwave-safe bowl is dry before adding the chocolate chips. Even a little bit of water can make the melted chocolate grainy.
* If the chocolate becomes lumpy, you may have overcooked it. Stir in 1 teaspoon of vegetable oil or coconut oil to make it smooth again.

Treats Prep

Be Safe

* Ask an adult for permission to use kitchen tools and ingredients.
* Ask an adult to help you use the microwave.
* Ask an adult for help when handling sharp or hot objects.
* Clean up spills right away.

Get Ready!

* Wash your hands.
* Clean your work surface before you start.
* Read the list of tools and ingredients for the sweet treat you are making. Set out everything you will need.
* Read the whole recipe at least once before you start.

What did the mother broom say to the baby broom at night?

"It's time to go to sweep!"

When You Are Finished

* Let hot treats cool completely.
* Put all the ingredients and tools away.
* Store leftover ingredients to use later.
* Wash all the dishes and cooking tools.
* Clean your work surface.
* Wash your hands before you eat your sweet treats!

Dirty Earwax Cotton Swabs

> How much does it cost a pirate to pierce his ears?
>
> **A buck-an-ear.**

Ingredients
* strawberry Pocky sticks
* mini marshmallows
* 12 soft caramel squares

Tools
* microwave-safe bowl
* spoon
* tray
* box of cotton swabs

EW!

1. Break the Pocky sticks near where the coating ends. Save the uncoated ends to snack on later.

2. Push a mini marshmallow onto both ends of each coated Pocky stick.

3. Follow the tips on pages 10 and 11 to melt the caramel squares.

4. Dip each mini marshmallow into the melted caramel.

5. Serve the earwax cotton swabs on a tray. For a more realistic effect, set a box of real cotton swabs on the tray too! April Fools!

What monster has the most fun on April Fools' Day?

Prank-enstein.

Sweet Mini Burger Surprise

Ingredients
- ½ cup chocolate hazelnut spread
- ½ cup powdered sugar
- ¼ cup shredded coconut
- green food coloring
- Hot Tamale candies
- Haribo Sour Streamers (orange)
- mini or regular vanilla wafers
- small tube of red frosting
- small tube of yellow frosting

Tools
- measuring cups
- bowl
- spoon
- sealable plastic bag
- knife & cutting board
- large plate

What do you call a vegan burger? **A mis-steak.**

YUM!

What did the tomato say to the other tomato in a race? **Ketch-up!**

① Put the chocolate hazelnut spread and powdered sugar in a bowl. Stir to make a **dough**.

② Divide the dough into 12 parts. Shape each part into a small hamburger patty.

③ Put the shredded coconut in a plastic bag. Add two drops of green food coloring. Seal the bag and shake it until the coconut turns green. This is the lettuce.

④ Cut the Hot Tamales and Haribo Sour Streamers to make tomato and cheese slices.

⑤ Set a vanilla wafer flat side up on your work surface. This is the bottom of the hamburger bun.

Continued on the next page. 17

6. Put red and yellow frosting on the wafer. This is the ketchup and mustard. Add some lettuce, tomato, and cheese.

7. Place a hamburger patty on another vanilla wafer. Turn them over and set them on top of the wafer from step 6 to complete the burger.

8. Repeat steps 5 through 7 to make the rest of the mini burgers.

9. Serve to friends on a large plate. Watch their faces as they bite into the sweet treats! April Fools!

What do you call fake spaghetti on April Fools' Day?

An im-pasta!

ORDER UP!

What do you call a cow that can't moo on April 1?
A Milk Dud.

Cat Poop Cookies

Ingredients
* 12 to 14 premade chocolate brownies
* 10-ounce container of chocolate frosting
* graham crackers

Tools
* large bowl
* spoon
* baking sheet
* parchment paper
* sealable plastic bag
* rolling pin
* shallow foil pan
* new, clean kitty litter scoop

OMG!

What do you call a magical poop?
Poo-dini.

What's a cat's favorite cereal?
Mice Krispies.

1. Put the brownies and frosting in a large bowl. Mix with a spoon and then **knead** to make a **dough**.

2. Line the baking sheet with parchment paper.

3. Pull off small pieces of dough to make cat poop. Poop comes in many different shapes! Roll some into logs and either leave them straight or bend them into curves. Form other pieces into balls or lumps. Place the cat poop on the baking sheet.

4. Put the baking sheet in the refrigerator for about 15 minutes.

5. Place several graham crackers in a plastic bag. Seal the bag. Crush the graham crackers with a rolling pin.

6. Put the graham cracker **crumbs** in the foil pan. Add more crushed graham crackers until the bottom of the pan is covered. This is the kitty litter and litter box.

7. Place the chilled cat poop brownies in the litter box. Roll some around so the kitty litter sticks to them.

8. Serve the cat poop brownies to your friends with a kitty litter scoop. April Fools!

Cockroach Crunchies

What kind of bugs smell the best?
Deodor-ants.

Ingredients
* bag of pitted dates
* 1 cup chocolate chips
* pretzel sticks

Tools
* knife & cutting board
* measuring cup
* microwave-safe bowl
* spoon
* baking sheet
* parchment paper
* plate

EEK!

What kind of bug is smarter than a talking parrot?
A spelling bee.

1. Cut several dates into thin strips. You'll need two strips for each remaining whole date. The strips will be the antennae for the **cockroaches**.

2. Cut a slit down the middle of each of the whole dates. These are the cockroach bodies.

3. Follow the tips on pages 10 and 11 to melt the chocolate chips.

4. Break pretzel sticks in half until you have as many halves as whole dates.

5. Line a baking sheet with parchment paper.

6. Dip a pretzel half in chocolate and place it inside a date. This will give the cockroach a salty-sweet crunch!

7. Use melted chocolate to stick two antennae to one end of the date.

8. Place the cockroach on the baking sheet.

9. Repeat steps 6 through 8 to make more cockroaches.

10. Place the baking sheet in the refrigerator for 15 minutes.

11. Move the cockroaches to a plate and serve them to your friends. Dare them to try one. April fools!

Cookies & Cream Rocks

Where do rocks like to sleep?
In bedrock!

Ingredients
- 10 to 12 Oreo cookies
- 12 ounces vanilla almond bark
- 7 ounces sweetened condensed milk
- ½ teaspoon cocoa powder

Tools
- large sealable plastic bag
- rolling pin
- knife & cutting board
- large microwave-safe bowl
- silicone spatula
- three small bowls
- baking sheet
- parchment paper
- plate or new, clean pail

WOW!

What do rocks eat?
Pom-e-granites.

24

1. Put the Oreos in a plastic bag. Seal the bag and crush the Oreos with a rolling pin.

2. Put the almond bark and sweetened condensed milk in a bowl. Follow the tips on pages 10 and 11 to melt them.

3. Put half of the Oreo cookie **crumbs** in the bowl of melted almond bark. Stir until smooth. Now it is cookies & cream **fudge**.

4. Put the cocoa powder in a small bowl. Put the remaining Oreo crumbs in a second small bowl. Leave a third small bowl empty.

Continued on the next page.

5. Divide the cookies & cream **fudge** equally between the three small bowls. Stir the ingredients in the first two bowls.

6. Line the baking sheet with parchment paper.

7. Pinch off pieces of fudge to make rocks in different shapes and sizes. Set the rocks on the baking sheet.

8. Place the baking sheet in the refrigerator for 15 minutes.

9. Serve the rocks on a plate or in a pail. Will your friends eat the rocks? April Fools!

It takes a *boulder* person to make this sweet treat prank!

COOL!

Knock, knock!

Who's there?

Justin.

Justin who?

Justin time for another April Fools' Day prank.

27

Keep Creating!

You've made some **delicious** treats with the recipes in this book! Hopefully you had some laughs with your friends too. But could you make any of the recipes differently? Could you use different ingredients? Or can you think of your own treat to fool your friends?

Do you or a friend have a nut **allergy**? Try making the mini burgers with plain chocolate spread instead of chocolate hazelnut spread.

Does a treat include an ingredient you don't like? Get creative! Find something else to use that you do like. For example, you could crush vanilla Oreos or vanilla wafers instead of graham crackers for the kitty litter.

How do you organize a space party on April 1st?

You planet.

Last Laughs

Which card in the deck is happiest on April 1?

The Joker.

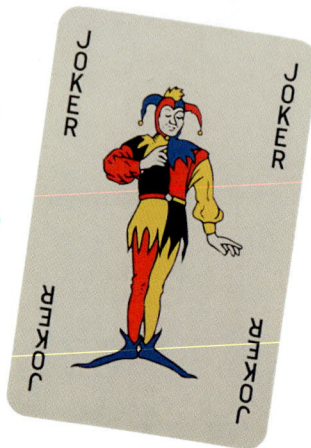

What did April Fools' Day say when it won an award?

Prank you!

Why was everyone so tired on April 1?

Because they just finished a long 31-day March.

What kind of rabbit tells April Fools' jokes?

A funny bunny.

Did you hear about the guy who lost the left side of his body on April 1?
He's all right now.

What did the ocean say to the beach on April Fools' Day?
Nothing, it just waved.

I played a prank on a skydiver on April Fools' Day.
He fell for it.

Did you hear about the cloud that tried catching some fog on April 1?
It mist.

Knock, knock!
Who's there?
Boo.
Boo who?
Don't cry, it's just an April Fools' joke!

Glossary

allergy – a sickness caused by touching, breathing, or eating certain things.

celebrate – to observe a holiday with special events.

cockroach – a large, brown insect that has long antennae, lives where it is warm and dark, and is mainly active at night.

crumb – a tiny piece of something, especially food.

culture – the particular behaviors, beliefs, art, and other products of a group of people.

delicious – very pleasing to taste.

dough – a thick mixture used in baking.

festival – a celebration that often happens at the same time each year.

fudge – a sweet, soft candy usually made with sugar, milk, butter, and flavoring such as chocolate.

historian – a person who studies or writes about history.

knead – to press, fold, and stretch something, such as bread dough.

practical joke – a trick played on a person or a group.

prank – a silly or mischievous act or trick.

tradition – a belief or practice passed through a family or group of people.